T0064588

RECOLLECTIONS

ED FLYNN

authorHOUSE®

AuthorHouse™
1663 Liberty Drive
Bloomington, IN 47403
www.authorhouse.com
Phone: 1 (800) 839-8640

Published by AuthorHouse 07/14/2015

ISBN: 978-1-5049-1960-9 (sc)
ISBN: 978-1-5049-1959-3 (e)

Print information available on the last page.

Any people depicted in stock imagery provided by Thinkstock are models, and such images are being used for illustrative purposes only. Certain stock imagery © Thinkstock.

This book is printed on acid-free paper.

Dedicated to Erin Elizabeth Elliott

Thanks to Jack Flynn editing
Cover art by (Silent Hero Studio logo)

CONTENTS

BULLETS AND BEER

When I was growing up in Chicago during World War II most kids had to entertain themselves. There were no theme parks like Disney World, or Disney Land. Kids pretty much went out and found their own entertainment

After the war the big attraction in our neighborhood was the International Amphitheater located on 42nd and Halsted at the eastern edge of the Union Stockyards. I understand it replaced a horse racing track that burned down and the Amp (as we called it) was built in 1937. The major show was the International Exposition and Stock show when cattle and horses from various locations in the far West and South were trucked into Chicago. This was the same Amp that the infamous Democratic National Convention of 1968 was held and orchestrated by Mayor Richard J. Daley.

In the Amp was the first time I saw a pretty girl wearing Levis. Levis were not common in the urban areas and that time and I became of big fan of that style of clothing, especially on girls.

I never paid to get into the Amp, nor did anyone that I knew of. The ability to sneak in to the Amp paid off later when I was asked to sell the New York Times at the Democratic convention.

We were always kept aware of the ongoing war from the reports coming over the radio and the fact that sugar was rationed and that was something I really missed.

In the window of a local butcher shop I saw a sign that showed tin cans entering the back of a machine gun. The sign said something to the effect that supplying tin cans to the military would help make bullets for the machine gun. That's all I needed, I borrowed a Radio Flyer wagon and walked through the alleys and collected tin cans for the war. I don't remember where I turned in the cans, but I felt I was contributing the war effort.

Living near the Union Stockyards was also interesting for a kid. I toured the slaughter houses and watched cattle being struck in the head as they walked through the entrance and were hung up and butchered. I also witnessed pigs being slaughtered as they were hung upside down, a man with a long knife slit their stomachs and they were pushed over a pool that contained boiling water to remove their hair and a pool collected their blood. At the end of the line, they were butchered. Someone told me not to watch the lambs being slaughtered as it was uncomfortable scene to witness.

The Stockyards looked like a lousy place to make a living. Herding the cattle and pigs looked like a hard job and working the slaughterhouses was also difficult. Upton Sinclair wrote about the slaughterhouses in 1906 it was called "The Jungle". He focused on the harsh conditions and the exploited lives of immigrants in Chicago and how the workers were treated and what they were exposed to. Readers, however, were more concerned on food safety as the novel's important issue. Lewis' book focused on the working class poverty, the lack of social supports and harsh and unpleasant living and working conditions. Much to Lewis' dismay, the government also focused on food safety and passed the Pure Food and Drug Act of 1906 it created the Food and Drug Administration. Sinclair was upset about the public's take on his book by saying. "I aimed at the public's heart, and by accident I hit it in the stomach."

There was a firehouse located at the entrance to the stockyards and on the walls were several pictures of firemen who had died while fighting fires in the Stockyards. Everything in the yards was made of wood and when a fire started it was a horror.

I heard about a fire in the Yards and ran to see it. I saw fireman returning from the fire as they were relieved by replacements and they looked exhausted. I came within two blocks of the fire and could go no farther as the heat was overwhelming. This was another tough job in the Yards.

There is a tavern in Bridgeport at 37th and Halsted called Schaller's Pump. It is the oldest tavern in the city as it has been there for 133 years.

Several years ago there was a brewery attached to Schaller's called Ambrosia Brewing Co. offering Ambrosia & Nectar beers. I toured this brewery as a young kid and watched the men working. They handed over a small container of beer for each visitor to drink. After about five of these beers I would leave the brewery one unsteady 10 year old.

I'll bet no one 10 years old is given a beer at Disney World!

Pick One:

1.) HIJACKED BY THE UNION JACK
2.) 31 FLAVORS
3.) UPSTAIRS OF THE VACANT LOT

During the late '60's I was driving a cab and I picked up a gentleman in downtown Chicago. He asked me to take him to Old Town. I drove straight down Wells St. and dropped him off at North Ave.

While cruising back toward the loop I noticed a young woman holding an infant in her arms. I was surprised as it was a very cold Chicago day in January.

She got into the cab and gave me an address in the Uptown neighborhood. I noticed she had a British accent. As we were talking I asked her how she liked living here in the United States and what did she find different from living in the U. K.

She said: Oh, you have so much of everything. I said: Like what? She said: Oh, you know, like ice cream. Ice Cream, I repeated, a little taken aback by her answer. She said: Yes, you have so many flavors. Well, I thought, I guess she is talking about 31 Flavors, the ice cream chain.

She was taking the baby to a doctor for an exam. When we arrived at her destination, she was rummaging through her purse and then said: "Oh my, I've forgotten my wallet." The cab companies would not get themselves involved in non-payment. They leave it up to the driver to contact the police.

She then said: "Why don't you stop by my house tonight and I'll give you your money." She then wrote down her phone number and address. I thought this was an okay deal and we said goodbye.

I thought I would do some reconnoitering and drive past her house to prepare for my evening visit. The address was something like 1415 North Wells Street. As I was driving along I saw the addresses: 1421, 1419, 1417 and then a vacant lot. I knew then that I had been scammed by the English girl. Then I remembered when I made the U-Turn to pick her up I noticed a brand new Yellow Taxi cab parked at the curb across the street from where she waved me down. Behind the wheel of the new cab was an older African-American driver. She assumed, correctly, that he would not be as good a candidate for the con as this Irish-American kid.

I didn't get laid, but I did get screwed.

A GREAT INFLUENCE

"Inculcating in the minds of our rising youth a love of the beautiful."
Oscar Wilde

Reading this quote caused me to reflect on the person who most influenced my life. I knew this person had to be the one who opened the world of theater to me. Her name was Lanny Sauris. She directed plays and musicals at St. Gabriel's, a Catholic school located in a lower working class neighborhood east the Chicago's Stockyards.

Lanny was a gifted piano player and directed several musicals. She encouraged the young people to act, sing and dance. She later encouraged people to direct their own shows and started a theatrical group called "The Theater Guild".

When I was about fourteen years old I tricked a friend into auditioning for an upcoming St. Patrick's Day show. This was an annual show put on by St. Gabriel's. I told my friend, Billy Cassidy, that I signed us up for an audition, but I just made that up. I knew that he would go along because his father was a talented singer and actor and Billy had a longing to perform.

Lanny warmly accepted us both, along with the other adult members of the group. My friend Billy went on to perform in several shows displaying a marvelous talent for the stage.

Lanny encouraged everyone to perform various roles and perform solos. My first solo was a song called: "Dapper Dan". I was a nervous wreck doing this song. I wound up with the nickname "Dapper Dan". But I gained more confidence in performing.

She encouraged us to write and direct shows. The first show I did consisted of scenes from "The Thurber Carnival" by James Thurber. I asked my brother to do a couple of Thurber's famous drawings on 2 x3 poster board and I set up them on stage. Lanny said nothing to me about the performance, except: "Who did those drawings?"

My love of theater is owed to Lanny Sauris as I have seen theatrical productions in Germany, London, Dublin, Stratford, Ontario and various American cities: Minneapolis, Milwaukee and New York.

I joined amateur theater groups and acted in plays at a local college. I also went back to St. Gabriel's Theater Guild to direct, write and act in several shows.

I discovered the great works of Shakespeare, Arthur Miller, Eugene O'Neill, G.B. Shaw, Tennessee Williams and Ibsen, to name but a few. I visited the home and museum of my favorite playwright, Eugene O'Neil, in Danville, California.

During a reunion show at St. Gabriel's I toasted my fellow actors and said: "These are our roots and this is what we will cherish for the rest of our lives." Everyone grew silent, and as one of the actors said later, that it was because they were emotionally touched and could not respond.

Lanny moved out of the neighborhood to be close to her only son and was never involved again in any shows. We named the theater after her. It is now called the "Lanny Sauris Theater" and the guild is still putting on shows.

Lanny died a few years ago and we held a memorial in her honor. Everyone held the view that she touched all of our lives by introducing music and theater to us, and we owe her, and honor her memory. I certainly do.

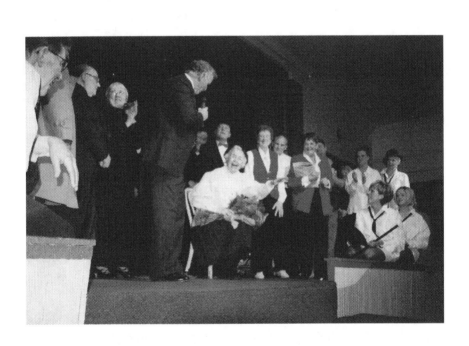

March 19, 2000

My dear friends,

How can mere words ever express my gratitude and appreciation for the wondrous, and loving tribute of last night? The memory will remain with me — shining bright and clear — in all the years to come.

I look forward to returning as a member of your audience, fondly and proudly cheering you on to great triumphs. God love you — I know — I do and always will.

With pride and affection,

Lanny

ETHNOCENTRIC

It was the summer of 1959 when Queen Elizabeth was visiting Chicago, and was escorted by the mayor, Richard J. Daley. I was listening to the event on BBC radio in Tumaco, Colombia. We were headed to a banana plantation just outside Tumaco, when the two owners of the plantation I was travelling with suggested we visit an English couple living in the town.

I was surprised and puzzled by the home they were living in. It was virtually a one-room shack. They were concentrating on the radio report of the Queen's visit. They did not speak about what they were doing in this part of the country. I was curious about why a couple from England would choose to live in a poor, rundown place like Tumaco. They both moved about the house as though it were a marbled palace, or an estate. Heads held high and jutting out their chins.

In the course of our visit the couple offered us a plate of fried bananas. What else? I often thought about this couple over the years as I got to know several different ethnic groups having worked as salesman for several companies in the steamship business soliciting import and export cargo. I worked for the Japanese, the Dutch, the Danish, the British and Koreans to name just some of the ethnic groups I encountered in my career.

I often heard about Americans who moved overseas for a job and were considered somewhat arrogant, or having a parochial attitude, whichever description one would use. But I found that this was not unique among Americans. If I spoke to a worker from Japan living in the United States I could sense a bit of a superior attitude with the man. In the early 1970's the Japanese economy was soaring. They were often cited as the country to imitate for their brilliant business acumen. This faded when their economy and influence started to fade. To this day the Japanese economy is struggling. If I mentioned someone who I thought was a bright person to the Japanese man, he would ask where this person was from. If he turned out not to be Japanese, he would dismiss the idea of someone not Japanese as being exceptional.

I was working for a Dutch steamship line and the New York office employed a few people from Holland. The Americans, working with them would say: "If you're not Dutch, you're not much." They experienced their arrogance first hand. Whenever the Dutch boss would visit the Chicago office, he lived up to their reputation. I heard that this Dutch boss once entered the head accountant's office and swept all the paper work off his desk. I guess this was to show he was unhappy with the man's method of accumulating paper work on his desk, and the Dutch manager considered the cluttered desk inefficient. He once complained to me that one of his young workers quit the job to take a higher paying job. He could not understand this man not wanting to stay with the company for less pay. He should have known that New York is a very expensive place to live.

But the biggest surprise I had with these foreigners was their attitude about women. I was riding in a car with a visitor from Japan who spoke excellent English. He started to tell me a joke: "What are the three worst things you would want in your life"? I asked him what they were the three worst things? He said; "A German boss, and English cook, and an American wife." We both laughed and then I said I could understand the first two inferences, but not the last one. He said: "oh you Americans, you let the women have far too much to say."

I would soon learn what he was implying when I was asked to have someone meet the flight of some men visiting from Japan who were arriving in the United States. Their plane was landing in San Francisco and I called the Oakland office to ask someone to meet the flight. The only person in the office was woman sales person, so I asked her if she could meet the flight, and she agreed.

I soon learned that when the two men departed from the plane they brushed right past the woman in a very brusque manner. They were insulted that a woman was assigned to meet their flight.

The next day my boss called me and said" "What were you thinking"? I said that I didn't understand the problem. He went on to tell me how the

Japanese think women are inferior and don't belong in the business world. Then I recalled that women, in Japan, were required to walk behind their husbands.

But the Japanese were not unique in their attitude toward women. I worked for a Danish company and the head office in Copenhagen notified us that they were sending a Danish woman to work with the Danish men in the California headquarters. The Danish men all laughed at this suggestion and when the woman arrived they treated her with disdain and little respect.

The Koreans were not at all different from the Japanese about their attitude toward women, as they also looked on them as inferior. I've heard that when a Japanese woman, or any women from the Far East comes to the United States to go to school, they are reluctant to return home as they realize what treatment awaits them.

There are many definitions of these traits shown by all ethnic groups: they are called prejudicial, partial, biased, ethnocentric, etc. There are an unlimited number of words to describe their views and attitudes.

The Germans had a reputation of being difficult people to work for, but they also had a reputation for being good business people.

But who were the most ethnocentric and insular of the group? I discussed this once with a woman who worked as an airline stewardess for SAS airlines. She said that she believed that the most arrogant and haughty people were the British. I agreed.

I thought about this and reached the conclusion that it was based entirely on their culture. The history of the British people is one that would create this attitude as they subjected many countries to become colonies of Briton. They had colonies in Egypt, Indian, Africa and the Far East. They used to say: "The sun never sets on the British Empire". British citizens who moved to these colonies expected to be treated like royalty. It's hard to blame them for feeling superior to the people subjected to their rule.

At home British upper-class is treated differently from the average Englishman. When World War I started it was reported that many upper class men joined the army and became officers. They were assigned several soldiers of the lower class to act as servants: Shine their boots, prep their uniforms and see to any of their personal needs.

During this war the pacifist philosopher, Bertrand Russell, was imprisoned for his criticism of the British government concerning the war. When he was put in jail he had been assigned to "First Division" which meant he would be treated in a manner suited to his social standing. He was allowed to wear his own clothes, rent a private room with his own books and furniture, eat his own food and employ other prisoners as servants. This practice has since been abolished.

The British have always been sensitive to any criticism about their class structure. An interesting note on this is when George Bernard Shaw wrote "Mrs. Warren's Profession". The play was banned by the Lord Chamberlain, an official theatre censor. The play was written in 1898, and it was not allowed to be performed in England until 1925.

What upset the people so much about this play? There is no mention in the play describing Mrs. Warren's profession, but she was a prostitute and later a madam running houses of ill repute in Europe. She returns to her home in England to visit her daughter, Vivie, who recently completed her studies at Cambridge. She is a bright and attractive girl and is being pursued by a couple of male suitors.

She learns how her mother has been earning her money and how she was able to support her during her school years. She wants to know her family history and discovers that her mother is not married, but uses the title of Mrs.

Another friend of her mother's tells Vivie that the young man, Frank, pursuing her may be her half- brother, the son of a local minister who may also be her father. It's is learned that Mrs. Warren was blackmailing the minister when she worked as a bartender in a local pub.

Her daughter now wants to know the details of her mother's life. Mrs. Warren goes on to explain that she worked in a pub long hours for little pay, and her half-sister died from lead poisoning while working in a factory. Mrs. Warren older sister talked her into becoming a loose woman.

Mrs. Warren's friend, Sir George Crofts, wants Vivie to marry him. He is twice her age, but says that upon his death, she will inherit his wealth, as well as carry the title of Lady Crofts. He also tells the young girl that he is part owner of her mother's houses in Europe. In our modern era this man would be called a pimp, as he is making money off the work of whores.

Vivie's, possible half- brother Frank, also wants to marry her as he has limited prospects and has already wasted his inheritance from his father. He is also worried that his two sisters will share in any money left after his father's demise.

Apparently this situation was not unknown in England at the time Shaw wrote this play. Many young girls did marry older men for the money and prestige and were encouraged to do this by their parents. Many women struggled to make a living and were exploited by the upper class. This was, no doubt, the reason the play was prohibited from being performed in England as it made the upper class uncomfortable.

I was surprised to learn that by the mid-1800s, most American states provided a free elementary education to the great majority of white children. In contrast, as late as 1870, only 2 percent of British 14-year olds were in school. I also learned that the United States was the first major country, in the 1930s, in which a majority of children attended high school. While as late as 1957, only 9 percent of 17-year-olds in Britain were in school. So I guess the conclusion should be drawn that it is a very elite society.

The British do like and respect the monarchy in the U.K. The queen no longer has any say in how the government is run, but the royal family is supported by the government for their lavish lifestyle. People in England, and around the world, are enamored by the royal family. They love hearing about the birth of the queen's great grandchildren and everyone likes to see the regal glamour displayed by the royal family and the stylish and beautiful gowns and robes worn by the royalty.

The English language alone will tell you about the number of names the British have come up with for naming and labeling the aristocracy. They have: nobleman, lord, lady, grand duke, duchess, duke, marquis, marquise, count, countess, earl, viscount and on and on.

Do the British deserve their reputation for arrogance and boastfulness? Let a British subject answer this question.

THE STATELY HOMES OF ENGLAND/
HOW BEAUTIFUL THEY STAND,
/TO PROVE THE UPPER CLASSES/ HAVE
STILL THE UPPER HAND.

Noel Coward

BATS, BANANAS AND BABES AND RIDING UNDER THE INFLUENCE

While visiting Bogota, Colombia with my friend Eduardo Rodriquez, he introduced me to his younger brother, Mario. Here was an example of a "what a small-world" as Mario attended college in Romeoville, IL and really mastered the English language. He talked like a guy from the old neighborhood.

Mario and a friend of his had several businesses going, such as a marketing firm in downtown Bogota and various agriculture enterprises. They said they were growing bananas on some property just outside Tumaco, Colombia. They asked if I would be interested in flying out there with them. I agreed to go along with them.

The year was 1959 and we flew off to Cali, Colombia and these two guys claimed the town was filled with pretty women. When the plane was landing in Cali, but still airborne, the propeller on one of the engines stopped. Mario's friend had been a pilot and he said not to worry as we were over the airport. My luck continues.

They seemed to be right about the women in Cali as I was watching all women walking on the streets of Cali and they were beautiful. Maybe it was the power of suggestion.

We then flew off to Tumaco and landed in a grass field. The town looked like an old west town as the streets were not paved and buildings were all wooden with sheet metal roofs. It rained every day in Tumaco and my two companions said this was why it was a great place to grow bananas.

I noticed several people in the town with one arm missing. When I asked why this was so, they said these guys hunt sharks with dynamite and sometimes the dynamite washes back into the boat. I could see people in the town selling pieces of shark butchered on a table.

Tumaco is located on the pacific coast of Colombia in the far southwest near the border of Ecuador the plans were to take a train into the jungle and there were only two trains a day as the tide would cover the railroad tracks during the day.

We spent most of the time drinking in a bar that had, like all buildings, a sheet metal roof. When the rain fell it was like sitting under the drums of Gene Krupa, the popular drummer in the 40's and 50's. By the end of the night we were pretty drunk and would go back to a hotel. The hotel was close to being like a garage and had windows with no glass.

When I entered the room I saw a bed with a table alongside with a candle burning. They told me that whatever I do, don't blow out the candle. When I asked why, they said because the bats will land on your neck in the dark. Needless the say, I never blew out the candle.

We overslept and missed the train into the jungle, so we went back to hanging out in the bar all day.

The next morning we again missed the train from drinking too much and over sleeping. Finally, we awoke in time to catch the train. When we arrived at the plantation I noticed the nice home they had built on the plantation to reside in while visiting. They had built a two story building with screens to keep out the bats they slept on the second floor to avoid any snakes entering the building.

We visited a lot of neighboring plantations that were deserted. They probably were unable to turn a profit and had to close them down. One plantation even built a small railroad with small rail cars to move the product around the plantation when approaching any bananas on the ground, I was to watch out as rats gather to eat the fallen bananas and the snakes show up to eat the rats.

I had only one encounter with a snake and fortunately I was on a horse that also spotted the snake. The ground was so wet from the daily rainfall that the horse was unable to bolt, as he was sinking in the mud half way up his legs. He tried to bolt and throw me, but I was able to hang on as the snake crawled away. My luck continues.

My friends also told me that the workers had no place to spend their earnings this resulted in someone building a bar in the middle of the jungle. We rode over to the bar one night. It was a bar with a thatched roof and no walls. The floor was probably five feet off the ground. I sat on the edge of the bar floor drinking several beers. I noticed a slight breeze on my face as though someone was fanning my face. My friends said that bats were hovering near me. I could not see them, which was okay with me.

On the ride home that night I was drunk and it was pitch dark. When horses know they are heading home they can't hold back their eagerness to run as fast as they can. My friends and I were riding on a narrow dirt road and the horses kept bouncing off each other. It was a miracle I didn't fall off the horse. The next morning I was looking into the horse's stall and noticed a bat hover near a horse. I've seen horses flick flies away from their bodies and figured the bat had no chance. But I was wrong, the bat gently landed on the horse's neck and stayed awhile, and when he flew off, I could see a stream of blood running down the neck of the horse. That could have been my situation except for the bright lights shining in the bar.

The next day we decided to hike into the jungle. We were accompanied by one of the workers who had a machete. It was a hand tool as the jungle grew so thick we could not walk through the trees. It wasn't until he cut down some of the growth that we could pass through. We walked for about an hour and came out on the Mira River separating Colombia from Ecuador. There was a family sitting in a thatched hut and looked surprised to see us. My friends noticed a small canoe that they called a mule. It was not big enough for all four of us to sit. One person had to stand in the canoe.

I was apprehensive about getting into this river as I witnessed wooden raft piled high with bananas moving rapidly in the river. I asked my friends if the raft was motor driven, and they laughed and said" "no it's the rapid current driving the raft." It turned out that the man carrying the machete was unable to swim, so he had to stand in the mule as we floated rapidly down the river. I was in a panic in the water and kept grabbing the rope attached to the mule, my friends hollered that I might tip the mule over and to let go of it. When the river made a sharp left turn we crashed into boulders on the shore and the pain in my legs was immense, but gave me a feeling of relief that I successfully got out of the rapid river. A few days earlier I was swimming in this same river and noticed how far out I was and realized that it was not my swimming that took me out this far, but the rapid current. I immediately headed back to the shore. My luck continues.

HOMELESS

"Nein, nein", they shouted at me. I was confused as to the reason my fellow pedestrians were upset while we waited at a cross walk in West Berlin for the light to change. I looked both ways, and did not see any vehicles approach in either direction. I proceeded to walk, much to the dismay of the German citizens, waiting with me. I learned that this was part of the culture of the German people, to adhere to all rules imposed by the authorities.

This idea was a defense for the German military and politicians at the Nuremberg trials. This was held after World War II. The defendants would respond to various charges of cruelty committed by saying: "we were only following orders". They meant orders could not be ignored.

Little did I know that I would suffer from this policy of the German people to follow all rules to the letter-of-the-law.

I was staying at a youth hostel in Frankfort, Germany. It was the middle of October and tourism declined significantly. The hostel was built by the American government who displayed a plaque inside showing the dedication by an American army general. The original hostel was bombed by the allies during the war.

It was a modest building with several triple decker beds inside dormitory rooms, and a shower room located on the first floor. It was somewhat empty, as there were few tourist registered.

I Was running out of money, and went to the railroad station to use their phones to call home. This was a large office with several phones that you paid to use for overseas calls. I phoned my mother and asked her to contact the neighborhood bank to transfer money to a bank in Frankfort. I knew that I would probably have to wait at least a few days.

For several days I stopped in the bank, and they had no record of receiving any money in my name. So I just stayed at the hostel waiting until my money arrived.

One morning I was checking in at the front desk to continue my stay. They normally do not let anyone stay beyond three days. The place was almost empty, so I did not think registering for another night would be a problem, but the clerk was adamant, I could not stay another day. I pointed out that there were a lot of empty rooms, but it mattered not, because he was "only following orders."

I did not worry, as there was another hostel located next to the train station called the "Bonhoff Mission." However, when I tried to register, they said they had no room. I only had a few deutsche marks, not enough to register at any hotel in downtown Frankfort.

As evening came, I started to worry. I walked all over town looking for some place to spend the night. While walking past a group of young guys who looked like "hippies" they offered me an apple. I took it, and wondered if I looked that desperate that I needed a handout.

I continued to walk around town, but when I passed a jewelry store, with a deep entrance-way, I could feel the warm air inside. There were a few people, mostly men and one woman sitting on the cement floor in the doorway. I refused to go inside, feeling superior to the poor homeless people sitting there. I continued walking, but when I passed the store for a second time, I changed my mind. I went inside, but refused to sit down, but after a while I grew tired, and sat among the group.

Just then, two drunken American soldiers passed by and were debating about beating an old man sitting among us. Thankfully, they changed their mind and moved on. The older woman discovered I was a foreigner, and started soliciting cigarettes, on my behalf, from people walking past our location.

Then one of the men discovered I spoke English. It turns out he was an American from a small town in southern Illinois. He came to Germany to do roof repairs. I soon discovered that he was an alcoholic, but he took me under his wing. He said the train station closes down every night to prevent people like us from hanging around. He said it opens at six o'clock, and we could go over to the station at that time. I mentioned to him that upstairs of the station was an office for making overseas phone calls. We proceeded to the station, and went upstairs. I pulled a large phone book out of a booth, put it on the floor, and fell right to sleep. I woke up when two Frankfort policemen were kicking my feet, and saying: "rouse", which did not require translation.

My homeless friend told me how unlucky I was, that just a few days earlier they were digging a hole in front of the station, and he said, he, and a few other homeless people, climbed into the hole and slept. He said it was comfortable, except some of the people passing by would spit inside.

By now it was early morning, and I told my friend that I was expecting money from home and we proceeded to the bank. They had my money, and I gave my homeless friend a few deutsche marks, and he quickly disappeared, no doubt to get himself some drink for the day.

I've never been homeless before, or since, but it was a great experience.

JUST ASK FOR A RAISE

My first job out of high school was working for a trucking company as a billing clerk (typist). I started out making $1.80 an hour, but shortly after being hired the office workers were represented by a union. The result was my pay being increased to $2.10 an hour. I was not that good a typist, but after typing for 8 plus hours every day my skill rapidly improved.

I was in charge of dispatching the trucks that hauled the freight to a midway point in Missouri. The freight was not always loaded by the time my eight hours expired, and as a result I put in a lot of overtime. This upset the management that consisted of two men. The terminal manager was a bit of a character as he probably wished he had become of a police officer. He had a red spotlight on his private automobile. He wore tinted glasses and spoke like a cop.

They called me into the manager's office and told me I was putting in too much overtime. I was confused, how could I leave after my eight hours when the dock workers were still loading the trailers and the drivers waiting to be dispatched. I feared being fired and started to punch-out earlier.

Later on I would learn what the real reason for their telling me I was putting in too much overtime: These two men would later lose their jobs for stealing. They announced their intentions to leave their job without any explanation to the staff. People were very emotional about them leaving the company. Some women even cried on their last day.

After a few weeks it came out that they were submitting false invoices for repairs on a tractor/truck for replacing the clutch. They submitted the same bill for the same truck numerous times. The headquarters in Wichita discovered the scam and fired them.

So the reason they told me I was putting in too much overtime was they were envious of my income. Why they didn't just ask for a raise was always a puzzle to me.

Later on in my working career I took a job as a freight solicitor (salesman) for a steamship company. One day I went into the boss's office and asked for a raise. This upset him. He said: "You know Ed, I was hired into this job after getting out of the navy in 1946 and I have never asked for a raise. He also said: "Do you know what I made in 1946?" I said: "No, but tell me what things cost then. Like a newspaper or a ride on a street car." He didn't seem to understand inflation.

Much later in the year the entire staff of the office went to a local bar to celebrate Christmas. The boss then told me a story about an embarrassing event in his career. Across the street from our office was a farm implement company called International Harvester, they did a lot of exporting to Europe and Asia and were a good customer. The boss entertained the export department staff of International Harvester by taking them to lunch at a night club called the London House. The London House was open for lunch and it was considered to be fashionable to eat there.

One afternoon after having lunch with the staff my boss said that same evening he was ushering at a White Sox game in Comiskey Park for extra income. Who shows up at the ballpark to be seated, but the same men he lunched with earlier. They were embarrassed, as was my boss. They made little eye contact.

I often wondered why he didn't just ask for a raise.

LUCK

The pilot for Colombia's Avianca Airlines announced on the intercom that he was returning to the terminal in Miami after taxiing the plane that was headed for Columbia South America. He said they were having problems with the radio and they would have this checked out before taking off. The year was 1959 and the plane was propeller driven as jet airplanes were not yet common.

I was 19 years old and was travelling with a native of Colombian, Eduardo Rodriquez Rubiano. He and I worked as billing clerks for a trucking company in Chicago. He was going to school at the U. of I., located at Navy Pier in Chicago. He was returning home for a visit and asked if I would care to join him. I had not travelled out of the country and all in my youth and thought this would be an interesting trip. It was.

When the plane returned to the terminal, several people exited the plane deciding against taking this flight out of the country. The pilot taxied out again on the runway and then made the same announcement about radio problems. Again we returned to the terminal and more people got off the plane. Eduardo said that the radio was probably not the problem that this was a common remark made by pilots when there are safety issues with the plane.

On a third approach the plane lifted off the runway and we were on our way to the first stop, Cartagena, Colombia. We landed and took off from Cartagena without any problems.

While flying out of Miami we flew directly over Cuba, which had recently completed a revolution putting Fidel Castro in control of the country.

We landed in Bogota and I was surprised how cold it was and then I learned that the city is located way up in the mountains and this causes the climate to be a bit chilly.

Eduardo was going through some issues with his wife who had two daughters from their relationship. Eduardo told me while living in an apartment building in Chicago, they suffered the loss of their young son who was playing in the hallway and got caught and killed in the elevator of the building. This, no doubt, put a severe strain on their marriage. Apparently he married his wife after getting her pregnant and it never seemed to be a good working relationship. The Columbian society was certainly class conscious and was noticeable when I arrived at Ed's home in Bogota. It was a large home with live-in maids who did the cooking and cleaning. Their work also extended to the point that they would be required to empty urinals it the bedroom of the men of the household in the middle of the night. A doorbell was alongside each bed and the occupant would not have to get up to go to the washroom.

Ed's wife was of a lower class than his family and this always seemed to be a major issue. Ironically we left Bogota to drive down to a town where Ed's mother-in-law owned and operated a hotel. This climate was much warmer, and more comfortable. But this was the first time I had seen homeless people. I would walk past closed stores late at night and see women holding infants in their arms while huddled in the doorway.

The hotel had a sidewalk café and when word spread that I was giving handouts to the poor people, a stream of people started to arrive at my table for donations.

One evening a friend of Ed's asked me if I remembered the flight number of the Avianca plane I flew in on. I said yes, I think it was flight 726. He then showed me a newspaper with the headline showing that plane had crashed in the Andes on its way to Peru. Someone at the table said that once Peru and Colombia got into a war, but it never proceeded as the planes from both countries never made it across the Andes'. I told Ed that I was thankful that he was from Colombia, and not Peru.

NEVER HEARD OF IT

It was 1956 and I was 16 years old and was walking along 42nd and Halsted Street where the International Amphitheatre is located, and they were preparing to host the Democratic convention for president of the United States. This was a rerun from the previous four years when Adlai Stevenson was running against the very popular ex-general Eisenhower.

A smartly dressed gentleman approached me and asked me if I was willing to go to work at the Democratic convention selling the New York Times. I never heard of the New York Times, but agreed to work for them nonetheless.

The Times' rep. asked if I could sell their papers inside the Amp (this is what we called the Amphitheatre) and double the price of the paper from five cents to ten cents. They said the increased price was due to the cost of flying the paper in from New York. I didn't see a problem with either issue, as I never paid to get into the Amp. for any shows in the past. I attended several shows at the Amp. – the major show being the International Livestock Exposition. This was an annual show and it was also where I saw for the first time pretty young girls wearing Levis.

I once came very close to being trampled by a team of Clydesdale horses as they were entering the arena pulling a Budweiser wagon. Otherwise, the shows were enjoyable.

I entered the Amp. without any problem and began selling the paper. When I informed some of the buyers that the paper actually cost ten cents, and not five, I had no problem with them. Until a Chicago cop who was taking a break and sitting in the stands asked for a paper. When he gave me a nickel and I told him the paper actually cost a dime, he put his foot in my chest and shoved me down the stairs.

My next encounter with a cop was when another cop called out and said: "Hey kid, did you hear they plan to nominate an Irish Catholic for the Vice President's position. I said I didn't know that and was surprised. I said: "what's his name?" and he said: "Jack Kennedy". I never heard of him, but being an Irish Catholic myself I was somewhat proud of this possibility. This may have been Kennedy's plan to test the political waters to see what reaction would result from the democrats considering the nomination of a Catholic for the VP position. Stevenson, however, went on to pick Estes Kefauver as his running mate. He would be defeated in his second attempt at unseating Ike.

The rest of the convention went on without any major incidents. But, when leaving the Amp., I noticed two older Black men picketing across Halsted Street carrying signs that read: "Jim Crow must grow." I heard of Jackie Robinson and Joe Louis, but I never heard of "Jim Crow".

Today I know about the New York Times and" Jim Crow" and the history of the hopeful Irish Catholic politician and Eisenhower's running mate, Richard Nixon. These two gentlemen would leave their indelible mark in history.

I once sent Maureen Dowd a note asking if she would be interested in meeting me for coffee, or lunch, or a drink in the evening seeing that I was a former co-worker of hers, but I never heard from her. She probably never heard of me.

THE NEW YORK, NEW YORK TIMES.
GET YOUR NEW YORK TIMES

AND THE WINNER IS

The Irish. They scored the highest! Are they actually the winners?

Well not so fast. I read some statistics in a book written by Patrick Moynihan and Nathan glazer called "beyond the melting pot" it presented statistics on the people living in new york: Puerto Ricans, Blacks, Jews, Italians and the Irish.

They listed alcoholism among various ethnic groups, and the Irish scored on top with 25%, while the Jewish people scored the lowest with 2%.

I was startled when I read that, but I soon realized that my definition of alcoholism, was somewhat skewed. When I was growing up, people assumed alcoholics, or drunks would wind up on skid row, on Madison Street, just outside the loop, where there were several hotels renting single rooms for one night. They were labeled S.R.O. hotels.

This meant they would be rented out mainly to bums living on the street. In my own neighborhood, we had "the bottle gang", a group of homeless alcoholics who hung in the alleys day and night.

So when I heard someone accused of being an alcoholic, is I assumed they meant: these homeless, hopeless people living on the street. If someone implied that someone I knew was an alcoholic, I would defend him by saying: "no, he couldn't be an alcoholic, he works full-time and never misses work."

I believed that people using the term alcoholic, were not aware of the social environment behind the habit of drinking alcohol. When I was growing up in the stockyards area we had a number of taverns along Halsted Street. They provided the workers with a place to cash their checks, grab a sandwich, and socialize. In my own neighborhood, we had many taverns that served multiple purposes, besides serving alcohol. For example; if you were arrested and needed $50 for bond money, you would call the local bar and they would send someone from to bail you out. If your car broke down, you could call someone at the bar to assist you. They always had someone there who could help.

It also worked as a "cracker barrel" in that you would get advice, or help with issues around the house, like plumbing, or carpentry, as they usually had someone hanging out in the bar who was a tradesmen. Political connections were also provided as well as information concerning employment.

As I got older, I realized that someone could lead a somewhat normal life, and still be an alcoholic. Drinking was such a part of the culture that it was hard to avoid it. Whenever someone came to your house it was expected that you offered them a drink. Almost all social occasions involved drinking. It was not unusual to see several people get drunk at wedding receptions.

I sat in on an alcohol intervention with one of my friends, and they put him in a rehab center for a week or two, and it didn't work. I understand these interventions have a very low success rate. I had to admit to myself, when his family was questioning him about his drinking, I could have changed places with him.

I quit drinking on my own, and needed no professional help, but I must admit that I regret a lot about my habit of over- drinking, as it led to some insensitive episodes in my life. I've talked to friends, who also quit, and they express similar regrets. Some experts also think that heavy drinking inhibits ambition, and that may be true.

As for Jewish people ranking at the bottom for alcoholism, I do wonder if this is the reason they historically have been successful in many areas, such as science, economics, law, medicine and education. They have won many Noble Prizes. They do, however, score high when it comes to being members of gamblers anonymous.

> God invented whiskey
> So the Irish wouldn't rule the world.

"When I read about the evils of drinking, I
Gave up reading." Paul Hornung
"I like a martini, two at the most.
If three I'm under the table
If four I'm under the host." Dorothy Parker

DIAGNOSIS

The year was 1950 and I was working at a newsstand at 47th and Halsted. This was a busy corner where workers coming home from the stockyards were boarding streetcars in various directions.

Someone approached me and told me that my father died. He was 44 years old was hospitalized for a week or so.

I heard various stories about his death. A nurse/nun reported that although my father was in a coma, he was rubbing the back of his neck. The nurse/nun said that this had to be very painful as they rarely see people in a coma experiencing pain.

I learned that the hospital suggested an autopsy. My family, for some religious reasons I guess, declined to have one performed.

My father's parents were still alive and sadly attended the wake. I was approached by a friend of the family who said to me: "Ed, your father was a very young man." I replied: "My father had gray hair". I suppose when you are ten years old, anyone with gray hair is considered old.

The funeral service was very stressful for my grandmother. When the funeral director was in the process of ending the ceremony, she prevented him from closing the lid on the casket. He tried several times before she finally let him close it.

I had mixed emotions about my father's passing. He was not a good or kind father. I witnessed him punching my older sister who was probably in her late teens. She was crying and looking stressed. He once showed up at my second grade class and took me in the hallway and proceeded to give me body punches.

I watched him once preventing my older brother Jack from leaving the house on a Saturday morning. Jack was headed down to his high school to try out for the basketball team. My father said" Where are you goin'? My brother told him, and my father said: "Sit down, you're not goin' anywhere." He was using his pseudo cop's voice and tone. This broke my brother's heart as he was a big fan of basketball and wanted to play for his high school. This was the way he always treated his children, asserting his authority for no rational reason we could understand. This was probably caused by his frustration at not becoming a Chicago cop, a dream of his.

Like a number of guys in my old neighborhood, he wanted that position of authority. He was a truck driver for the Railway Express Company and always referred to himself, not as a truck driver, but a chauffeur. When he would stop at our house in the course of the day, we would see his truck and run home. He didn't think we should be out playing in the daytime, but sitting at home. We never could understand his reasoning.

The nearest he ever came to being a cop was when his cousin became Sheriff of Cook County. His cousin's name was Elmer Walsh and he beat out a Democrat named Richard J. Daley. My father expected to be made a cop for the sheriff's department, but it never happened. Instead they gave his younger brother, Ed, the job.

My father probably made a good living driving a truck, but he never brought the money home. When he died, a loan company showed up at the house saying he owed them money. They were told they were out of luck.

Not too long after the funeral someone asked my grandparents if my dad had any health issues as a young boy. They said" "Oh yes, he had seizures." When asked what was the cause. They answered: "The devil."

Seeing the way he treated the members of our family and neglected his duties as a father, I now think the diagnosis was probably not far from the truth.

THE BOTTLE GANG

I have always been a bit confused about the definition of an alcoholic. When I was growing up in the Stockyards area, we had a group of men we called "the bottle gang", or "wineos", or "barflies". These men were probably in their 30s 40s and 50s and would lie up against a garage in our alley looking tired. We would play with these guys inviting them to participate in a softball game. The pitcher would pretend to make a pitch, without the ball, and the bum (as we would call him) as the batter would swing thinking he was swinging at the ball. We would all laugh.

The apartment building we lived in on 47th street had a front hallway leading up to our second-floor apartment. In the winter we would have to walk past men sleeping on the stairs. It was one of the places they escaped our Chicago winters.

This was what I thought defined an alcoholic. When someone would say that so and so was an alcoholic I would protest the remark saying that the man held a full time job and never missed work. It never occurred to me that someone could be an alcoholic and maintain a job. Certainly the "bottle gang" did not have jobs.

"Skid Row" was the term they used to describe west Madison Street in downtown Chicago where a group of men would sit on the curb outside of Single Room Occupancy (S.R.O's) apartments that could be rented out for a very small amount of money. Many of these men would sleep in these single occupancy rooms. A friend of mine in high school once occupied a room in an S.R.O. on Madison Street after his parents' marriage had broken up. He said one morning he tried to use the bathroom to shave when he noticed a lot of blood on the sink and mirrors. He thought it would be best not to shave that morning. When he arrived at school, they expelled him for not shaving. He never explained the situation to authorities and was not allowed to participate in the graduation ceremonies. He asked me about the graduation and I was confused, thinking he was there. He said: "No I was not. I had joined the Army by then."

I worked in the steamship freight business as a salesman and we would take clients to lunch and dinner and, of course, we would drink to excess. So if a salesman would be seen at work having drunk too much it was not considered inappropriate, or unusual.

I once heard about a guy who also worked in the steamship business. He drank in the bar located at ground level of his high rise office. He would stay in the bar until it closed and then would then go into his office and sleep on the desk. This, apparently, did not bother management.

"The nameless, useless nobodies who sleep behind the taverns, who sleep beneath the EL. Who sleep in burnt-out buses with the windows freshly curtained; in winterized chicken coops or patched-up truck bodies. The useless, helpless nobodies nobody knows: that go as the snow goes, where the wind blows, there and there and there, down any old cat-and-ashcan alley at all. There, unloved and lost forever, lost and unloved for keeps and a day..."

"There where they sleep on someone else's pool table, in someone else's hall or someone else's jail, there where they ...they sleep the all-night movies through and wait for rain or peace or snow, there, there beats Chicago's heart."

Nelson Algren "Chicago City on the make"

I recently read an article about Staten Island, NY where many, many people are overdosing on prescription drugs and "one or two storefronts that look no different from the rest also do a steady word-of-mouth business in illegal sale of OxyContin, oxycodone, Percocet and other prescription painkillers, A neighborhood ice-cream truck playing its jingle might also be selling pills. A window-blinds and drapery store sold oxycodone pills."(New Yorker September 8th, 2014.)

The article noted that drug overdoses overtook car accidents as the leading cause of accidental deaths in the United States in 2014. Overdose victims are between the ages of thirty-five and fifty four. It has also been reported that suicides now exceed deaths from auto accidents. Could this all be related to drugs and alcohol abuse?

When I was growing up drugs were not an issue, but Nelson Algren noticed on the North side, that drugs were also a problem, as well as alcohol.

I also heard when I was growing up that no one could become an alcoholic just drinking beer. Well, that turns out not to be true.

So why does society turn its back on this social problem? I guess some people try to address it, like Alcoholics Anonymous. But A.A. and other intervention programs have a very limited success rate.

The question is: why do people feel a need to get drunk, or get high?

I once worked for a man who told me he quit drinking and then returned to drinking. When I asked him why, he said he didn't know what to do with himself. He sat at his kitchen table with nothing to do. He provided a clue when we discussed a company situation. I never met the management from New York, as the boss always insisted we salesmen be out of the office with the appearance of calling on customers. Another salesman joked that I was like Ensign Pulver from the movie "Mister Roberts". The boss, having served in the Navy during World War II was offended that this man gave me the title of Ensign. He kept asking why the man referred to me with that title. My guess was that he never achieved any rank with the Navy during his service and was offended that a young salesman would receive such a title, even unofficially.

The man said: "Oh, you know, that's from the movie: "Mr. Roberts". My boss, the ex-sailor, had never heard of the movie.

This is my point. Some people never develop an interest in anything and feel a need to consume alcohol to feel better about their lives. They don't read, they don't attend movies, or see plays. Their only interest is in drinking, or drugs to make them feel less stressed, pseudo-happy.

Do we still have "bottle gangs" or "wineo's"? We do, but now we refer to these people as "homeless". Many parts of our country experience a lot of homeless people. The latest statistics show we have 600,000 homeless people in the United States. This is a problem in warmer climates like Southern California where it is much easier to sleep outside, versus sleeping outdoors in Chicago in mid-winter.

It was reported that the authorities in Florida arrested a man for giving food to the homeless. Instead of helping these people, the establishment would rather discourage everyone from helping them.

Here is a quote from Pete Hamill who wrote a book about excessive drinking. He witnessed a lot of people in his neighborhood drinking to excess. "Most of the time he was just another one of those quiet wounded men who live out their lives in bars." ("The Christmas Kid")

THE BROGUE

I was driving a taxi cab in Chicago and one afternoon I picked up a British businessman at the Prudential Building. We were only a few minutes along when he asked me: "How long have you been here"? I didn't understand the question and asked him what he meant. He said: "When did you come from Ireland"?

I said: "Oh no, I'm not from Ireland I was born here." He said: "Oh, I understand, your parents are from Ireland." I said" "No, they were born here as well."

It was now getting to become a common occurrence that I seemed to have an accent, or a brogue, as they call it. I once was visiting my doctor's office and he had a nurse from South Africa. She lived in England for a while prior to coming to the States. When leaving the office one day, she said something about us being fellow citizens. I didn't know what she meant, and she said: "oh you Irish, you know I mean we are both from the U.K." I said: "I'm not from the U.K." She responded: "okay, okay you're from Ireland and isn't that part of the U.K.?" I again responded that I was not born in Ireland that I was born in the United States. She was surprised and said that the elevator starter in the building was from Ireland and when I get down to the lobby I should ask him to listen to me speak and see if he thinks I'm from Ireland.

I approached him and asked if he knew the nurse upstairs and he said he did. I then asked him if he could tell where I was from. He said: "talk a little more." I did, and then he said: "It's either Cork, or Kerry, I'm not sure which county."

I have an older brother and he is never questioned about having a brogue. My twin sister, Mary, is also asked what county she is from. She is a member of an Irish Club called "Galic Park" and she is quite often asked what county she is from. I think I may have developed this accent from spending time with my fraternal grandmother who was from Ireland. I remember visiting her as a young boy and I brought a friend with me. She asked my friend several questions about his family and every time my friend would give me a puzzled look as he could not understand her. She would ask questions such as what his father did for a living, and where exactly did he live in the neighborhood. After a while I quit translating and would answer the questions myself. She said: "why can't he answer me."? I said: "he can't understand you." She said: "why"? I said: "because of your brogue." She said: "I don't have one." She had been living here for close to fifty years and didn't think she had a brogue.

My son Kevin has an Irish band and he said people often ask him when he came here and he has to tell people he is not from Ireland. They think he has a brogue. He is only half Irish as his mother is Polish. So perhaps he inherited my accent. At least he inherited something from me. But I must remember the advice my grandmother always gave me when she would say: "don cha be talkin."

THE CAVALRY

My friend at work, Eduardo invited me to visit his home in Colombia. He had a relative who was an officer in the Colombian army. He was a high ranking officer; he took me and Eduardo with him one day when he went on his rounds visiting military sites in Bogota.

We visited an Officers Club and it was impressive for its image of gruesome harshness. The military officers appeared to be very tough guys. This was five years prior to when the guerilla movement, known as FARC, started. FARC is still active today and uses kidnapping, drug trade and various other harsh means to support their revolution.

In 1959 the Colombia military still had a cavalry. It made sense when you see the rough terrain of Colombia. Riding horseback at that time seemed to be the best method of traveling in combat missions.

Eduardo's officer relative invited us to visit the cavalry headquarters. Eduardo made the mistake of saying that he was an experienced rider and could handle any horse without difficulty. This officer saw to it that the roughest horse in the stable was brought out for Eduardo. When we arrived we saw four soldiers trying to bring out a horse that was nearly uncontrollable. They were hanging on this horse with all their might trying to calm him down so Eduardo could mount him. Eduardo never did get on the horse as he realized this horse was too much for any human rider.

The officer invited his wife and her cousin to join us and we each were given a horse to ride. These horses were very big and well groomed and were fitted with English saddles. Riding with these types of saddles resulted in not actually sitting on the horse's back, but forced to you ride like a jockey with your feet in the short stirrups. The two women and I took the horses out on the trail. These horses wanted nothing to do with casual riding as they were eager to move at a rapid pace. I had no experience riding horses, having grown-up in Chicago, but I was forced to hang on and learn to handle the fast moving horse. Then the women were having trouble as the horses started to rear-up causing the women to become frightened. I was forced to dismount and try to calm the other two horses. I was holding on to their reigns while they reared up in excitement. I was able to calm the horses down and we decided to return to the stable. Here I was a young guy with no real experience riding horses trying to protect the young women riding with me. I must say I was relieved when we returned the horses to the army's stable. Eduardo never did ride that day and was humbled by his boasting about being an experienced horseback rider.

THE FAITH HEALER

I scheduled a Sunday afternoon to see both a play and attend a friend's wake. I wanted to see "The Faith Healer" a play written by Irish playwright named Brian Friel as I was big fan of his work.

I attended a matinee and afterwards went to the Southside to attend the wake of an old acquaintance of mine named Pat. I had acted in plays with him and I was surprised when I heard he had died suddenly. I had not seen him in a few years. When I approached the casket I was greeted by a young woman, his daughter. I extended my sympathy. She said: "Oh yeah, we wonder what would have happened if he had not gone to the faith healer.

I asked her to explain. She said her dad and a friend attended a session with a Catholic priest who claimed to be a faith healer. I assumed this was cause of his death. I repeated my condolences and went to the rear of the funeral parlor to see if I could get a further explanation of what happened. I met some friends and they explained, in detail, the events leading to Pat's death. It turned out that the he had arranged for a friend of his to attend the session with the priest because his friend was dying of AIDS.

The faith healing session was originally scheduled in the local Catholic Church that we all attended as youngsters, but the pastor refused to allow the priest to hold his faith- healing program in the church. They then moved the session to a local bakery that provided a suitable area to hold the event.

The priest had all the participants seated alongside each other. For some reason, Pat also became a participant and was seated along with his friend and the other people partaking in the program.

44

The priest moved along laying his hands on each person and reciting prayers. When he laid his hands on Pat, Pat fell to the floor. People rushed to assist him but the priest told them not to worry that this was common and Pat would be fine in a short while. The session went on and Pat never moved. Finally they called for paramedics and they discovered Pat had died of a heart attack. A few years later I attended the wake of Pat's friend who finally died from AIDS.

I thought about Brian Friel's play and was thinking at the time about the people showing up for the faith healing session. In the play the people were described as being very ill and seemed to have little hope of recovering from their plight. I suppose this was the reason Pat wanted to take his friend to see if the priest could relieve him from his battle with AIDS. I also thought that the pastor of the church refused to allow the sessions to be held in the church said a prayer of thanks for his enlightened decision.

This certainly was a case of art truly reflecting life as we know it.

Quoted from FAITH HEALER BY Brian Friel

"Faith healer-faith healing. A craft without an apprenticeship, a ministry without responsibility, a vocation without a ministry. ...And occasionally it did work. Oh, yes. And when it did, when I stood before a man and placed my hands on him and watched him become whole in my presence, those were nights of exultation...But the questionings, the questionings. 'Am I endowed with a unique and awesome gift?' My God, yes, I'm afraid so. And I suppose the other extreme am I a con man?-which of course was nonsense, I think."

THE MERCHANT
OF VENGENCE

While touring London in the 1970's I visited museums and saw a few plays. I saw the long-running play "The Mouse Trap" by Agatha Christie and "Sleuth" by Anthony Shaffer. The first Shakespeare play I saw was in Dublin, Ireland. The play was "Macbeth" it was well done and I became a fan of Shakespeare.

While in London I planned to see "The Merchant of Venice" at the National Theater. I left the hotel late and when I exited the subway I saw a crowd waiting for the elevator to take them up to street level. I took the stairs, not aware that I was six floors underground. Because I was late for the play I did not get a program and did not know the names of the actors performing the play. I got a program during intermission and Shylock was played by Laurence Olivier. I thought he was excellent in the part.

"The Merchant of Venice" is a difficult play as it has some harsh anti-Semitic language. Jewish people are offended by the language and they should be. A friend of mine visited Stratford, Ontario to see some Shakespeare plays and said he was uncomfortable watching "The Merchant of Venice" because he was with a couple of Jewish friends. I saw the same play and agreed that I also would have been uncomfortable.

Very often the theater in Manhattan's Central Park will produce this play causing the Jewish population to be offended, but any protest of the play results in increased attendance. Recently an opera called "The Death of Klinghoffer" opened in New York. It is based on the killing of a Jewish passenger aboard a cruise ship. He was confined to a wheelchair and was shot and pushed overboard. People in New York saw the theme insensitive and insulting. People protested the opera, but it got attention and increased attendance.

I read that an Irish actor was one of the first to play Shylock as serious and dignified. I was puzzled until I read an explanation by Harold Bloom, who is considered an expert on Shakespeare and has taught at Yale for a number of years. Bloom says that Shakespeare wrote "The Merchant of Venice" as a romantic comedy. It is hard to view this play as a comedy. But Bloom goes on to explain that Shakespeare wrote it to contrast it with Marlowe's "The Jew of Malta."

Bloom writes in his book: Shakespeare: The Invention of the Human: "One would have to be blind, deaf and dumb not to recognize that Shakespeare's grand, equivocal comedy "The Merchant of Venice" is nevertheless a profoundly anti-Semitic work."

Shylock was originally played as a vaudevillian character wearing a red wig and probably a fake nose and talking with a Yiddish accent. He was similar to Dickens' Fagin in "Oliver Twist'.

Bloom, however, does not see Shakespeare as anti-Semitic, but does consider the play to be anti-Semitic. He writes: "Shakespeare would exclude the possibility that he was personally either anti-Semitic or philo-Semitic," Bloom explains that there were very few Jews living in London at the time Shakespeare wrote his play because so many were driven out of England 300 years before.

Several years after my London visit I met Bloom at a book signing. He autographed my book and I asked how the Oxfordian theory started that claims Edward de Vere, 17th Earl of Oxford (1550-1604) was the true author of Shakespeare's plays and poems? He sighed and answered: "If I tell you the name of the man who originated this idea, it will explain it all. His name was Looney," That settled it for me.

Bloom ends his chapter on "The Merchant of Venice" with the following: "I end by repeating that it would have been better for the last four centuries of the Jewish people had Shakespeare never written this play. So shadowed and equivocal is "The Merchant of Venice", though, that I cannot be certain that there is any way to perform it now and recover Shakespeare's own art of representing Shylock."

In the National Theater's performance all the actors wore formal mourning clothes. Bloom must have seen this production as he thought this was absurd. He also did not like Olivier's performance as he wrote: "I could never come to terms with Olivier's suave philo-Semitic Shylock, who seemed to emanate from Freud's Vienna not at all from Shakespeare's Venice. The top hat and black tie had replaced the Jewish gabardine, and the powerful speeches of menace were modulated into 'Civilization and its Discontent's.'"

Performing the play now, as Shakespeare wrote it, would be impossible as it would be perceived as more offensive and anti-Semitic. Playing Shylock as a comic, or a buffoonish character would be a disaster.

Many playwrights see comedy much differently. The old saying that comedy is tragedy revisited is true. Eugene O'Neil was challenged to write a comedy and wrote "Ah, Wilderness". This play, like Shakespeare's "The Merchant of Venice" is hard to view as a comedy. From O'Neil's perspective having a sober father, a drug free mother and the only drunk in the family is a comical uncle, was comedy to O'Neil.

O'Neill said that at an age when most young men were romantically in love with a "pure girl," he was a Broadway wise-guy. He also commented on Ah, Wilderness: "many people said that I had written about my adolescence. The truth is that I had no youth, Ah, Wilderness was nostalgia for a youth I never had."

The young man in the play (possibly O'Neil) received a lot of attention from his parents and they prepared to celebrate the 4th of July with a lunch. O'Neill shows us a mythical family that is not at all like his. To see the family life he experienced you would have to see O'Neil's "Long Day's Journey into Night".

Edward Albee's play "Who's Afraid of Virginia Woolf" is comical by its absurdity. George and Martha are bitter alcoholics and have a mythical child. Later in the play George says their son died in a car crash. Martha is upset by his comment, even though their child does not exist.

After seeing August Strindberg's play "The Dance of Death" I felt the play influenced Albee's writing of "Who's Afraid of Virginia Woolf". It also influenced O'Neill's play writing. O'Neill said: "the discovery of August Strindberg led him to start writing plays" (Stephen Black, Eugene O'Neill, Beyond Morning and Tragedy p.134)

I met Albee once and asked him a question while he signed a copy of his play, but he gave me a grumbling inaudible answer. It would not have been a good idea to ask if Strindberg's play influenced his writing. "The Dance of Death" is comical especially when listening to the man and his wife's quarrelsome remarks. This is another example of some playwright's idea of comedy.

I attended an interview with the composer and lyricist Stephen Sondheim where he told the story of his mother, Foxy, (her maiden name was Fox) who wrote him a letter saying: "The only regret she ever had was giving him birth." Sondheim told this story as if it were humorous. With the passing of time, I suspected that he viewed this cruel remark as a joke. Perhaps Sondheim and Albee should consider writing a play about Sondheim's mother and call it "Dear Mother Foxy". Sondheim could turn it into a musical. He harbored antipathy toward his mother and refused to attend her funeral. Albee did not see his mother for 17 years.

THE ICEMAN WILL NO LONGER COMETH

In the 1940's I asked my mother why she never baked a pie, or a cake? "You know we're in the middle of a war and they are rationing sugar." I asked the same question when the war ended, and she said: the oven is broke. It wasn't.

It took me a while to figure out my mother's aversion to home appliances. We, like many of our neighbors, had an ice box. She would order a 25 pound block of ice from our iceman, Mr. Harrington, at least twice a week. The ice would only last a few days, and then we would be without it. It didn't matter much as we had nothing to refrigerate.

Then we bought a refrigerator. I thought we were moving up in the world, how modern a family we were becoming! One day I invited a classmate home and I proudly showed him our new refrigerator. When I opened it, there was nothing inside. It was completely empty. He was puzzled and asked why there was nothing in there. I didn't understand the question, as we never ice boxed anything in the past, why should owning a refrigerator be any different.

Another chore to be avoided was cleaning the house. My mother did not wash the dishes, she would say: "I rinched them". She cleaned the kitchen table by sweeping off any of the crumbs onto the floor. Our very thin dog, Jeff, appreciated this as it was his limited chance to eat something. Because of her domestic cleaning policy we always had mice. The mice were such a familiar sight around the house that we named them. We called them Pixie and Dixie two mice featured in a cartoon shown on television. She always faulted the neighbors for this rodent problem, but years later when she moved we discovered two mice in her new apartment. We told her that Pixie and Dixie had followed her.

My mother believed all domestic chores were something to be avoided. There was a large grocery store (not a supermarket) a few blocks from our home, but we rarely bought food there. My mother would have us buy the food on a daily basis at a small grocery store across the street just minutes before supper. Mrs. Kennedy, the owner, was so pleased to have us as steady customers that she even allowed us to run a tab. When we moved a few years later, she wept. I suppose that Mr. Harrington, the iceman, also wept when the era of delivering ice ended. Years later my sister-in-law questioned my mother about her younger life and asked what she wanted to become when she was growing up. Her answer: "a dancer". I was not surprised, as it was my mother's favorite pastime was singing at a piano bar. She even got up to sing in front of a large crowd celebrating her 75th birthday.

I have a twin sister which caused several people to ask my mother who I looked like. They said: "Mary looks a lot like your husband, John, but who does Eddy look like?" She would answer: "Mr. Harrington!"

Years later when she was in a nursing home I visited her and told her that I changed my name. She asked what I was talking about. I said I no longer go by the name of Edward James Flynn, but E. Harrington Flynn, a man from the ice age. She gave me her usual look of: I think you're crazy!

THE TERRORIST

Being a strange person, I have strange hobbies. One of them is when I travel I visit universities in the town I'm visiting.

My friend, Moe, and I travel a lot and visit universities. We once were in Northern California and visited the campus of Stanford University. On the campus was a replica of Rodin's "The Gates of Hell". Each of us posed for a picture in front of the structure as if we were saying goodbye to the other as he was entering hell. He struck the identical pose. In real life, we may both end up in hell.

We use these visits to impress mostly strangers by saying things like: "We went to Stanford together". We never explained that we were just tourist, and not students. People who know us don't bother asking for any details.

I have a feeling that my poor dressing habits have led to my being a crime suspect. I once stood in front of Fannie Mae candy store just prior to Valentine's Day. I was window shopping for some candy for my wife. I was wearing a navy pea coat and wool stocking cap. When I entered the store I noticed the two women clerks looked distressed. When I ordered the candy, they let out a sigh. I asked what the problem was. They said they thought I was casing the store to hold it up.

I deposit a check once a month in my local bank, and whenever I enter the bank I am always confronted by an employee wanting to know if they can help me. I always tell them no, but they continue to ask if I need assistance. I was watching a television show about bank robberies. They said banks no longer hire security guards with guns as they are afraid some innocent person could get shot. Instead they confront anyone suspicious alerting them that they have been inspected and viewed. Now I deposit my check and leave the bank as soon as I can.

There used to be a restaurant in my neighborhood with a public phone in their lobby. One night I pulled my car up to the front of the restaurant to use the phone and I saw the owner viewing me and he ran from behind the counter and locked the door. I guess I looked too dangerous to use his lobby phone. Now I have a cell phone and don't need his lousy phone.

In my bearded days I flew to Europe once on Icelandic Airlines. The flight to and from Europe both stopped in Iceland and in the flight brochure it said passengers could visit Reykjavik between flights. When I tried to arrange this with an agent for Icelandic in London, he danced around the issue saying it would not be possible for me to do this. I think he was instructed not to let any hippie characters into the city.

While traveling in Ireland I in 1970 met a fellow American tourist and asked him what he saw so far in Ireland. He mentioned being in Northern Ireland and I was considering going there myself. He said he was in of Londonderry when a store widow was blown out by an explosion. He said he was very afraid and ran down the street. He said he thought this was a mistake because maybe people thought he was the cause of the explosion and would pursue him. I made-up mind right there not to even comes close to visiting Northern Ireland.

A Canadian friend of mine who taught at a small college in Memphis mentioned that he went to school at the University of London. I was writing him from time to time, about my trip in Europe and thought it would be interesting to visit the campus of the University of London. I was on the campus for about five minutes when I had to use the restroom. I was washing my hands when I was confronted by a security guard who asked me what business I had being on the campus. I told him I was just visiting the campus and he insisted I leave immediately. I guess having long red hair and a red beard alarmed the security office when they spotted me on the campus. Do you think they thought I may have been a terrorist from the IRA?

I cannot understand the image I portray to other people. One of the most embarrassing and puzzling situation I encountered was leaving a meeting at the Ethical Humanist society. I took my coat off the rack and as soon as I left the building a young woman came out and asked me if that was my coat I was putting on. I told her that I did indeed own the coat and she just looked at me with a skeptical look on her face. Did she think I was unethical?

Moe Farnan and Ed Flynn on the campus of Stanford Univ.
Standing in front of a replica of Rodin's "The Gates of Hell"

THREE WOMEN
PASSENGERS AND A VET

I picked-up an older woman on the near north side of Chicago and she asked to be taken into the loop. This woman, who was probably in her 80's, had a French accent, somewhat rare in Chicago. She started to talk about her past. She said she had met her husband in Paris at the end of World War I. He was an officer in the United States Army. She described what a dashing figure he made in his highly polished boots and impressive military uniform. She talked about him in the past tense so I assumed he must have died. While she spoke of him she had a shy smile on her face and the cab interior seemed to develop a dim glow. When we arrived in the Loop she seemed reluctant to end the talk of her late husband. He must have been an impressive man for her to leave her home and family and move to the United States with him.

She smiled a sad smile and wished me a good day. Bon Jour.

I picked up an older Black woman outside a grocery store along the South Side of Halsted Street. She had a lot of packages and she was carrying a baby. She looked exhausted. She was slumped in the back seat during the entire ride. When we arrived at her home I asked her if I could assist her in bringing up her packages. She instead handed me the baby to carry up to the second floor. Seeing an older woman with a very young infant was not unusual in the Black neighborhoods as many young girls gave birth to babies only to pass them on to their mothers, grandmothers, or aunts to raise. Today this is common in many middle class neighborhoods as young girls must work or continue school and let the task of raising their offspring to an older woman.

I dropped off two guys in Hyde Park and decided to cruise back toward the Loop. Then I was hailed by a Black woman who appeared to be very old, possibly in her eighties. She got in the cab and gave me an address that was a very short distance away. I couldn't blame her, as walking even that short distance was probably a major challenge.

I didn't drive more than a block and a half before arriving at her destination. It was such a short trip that I didn't turn on the meter. When she was ready to exit, she opened her purse and asked what the fare. I said there would be no charge. She burst into tears and started to sob. I was taken aback by this and asked what was the problem? She said: "Oh I know, you thought I was going to rob you. "I tried to reassure her that this was not the case, but she continued to cry as she exited the cab. I suppose if I were robbed this is the person I'd select to perform the act. I couldn't have felt any safer.

I picked up a Black soldier at the O'Hare airport. He told me he had just returned from the war in Viet Nam, which was still going on. The address the soldier gave me was a public housing complex on the near north side of Chicago. He seemed happy to be home and was smiling and talking during the entire trip. When we arrived it didn't seem inviting. It was a warm summer day and a great many kids were playing on the balconies. It sounded like a bee hive. I was struck by the cruel irony of this soldier coming home from defending our country and having to live in such grim housing. I shook his hand and thanked him for the service to our country.

BROKEN LEG, BROKEN DOCTOR

I was 6 years old and my 18 year old sister Betty was assigned to watch me and my twin sister while my parents went out for the evening. Betty invited her boyfriend to assist in watching us.

I was playing outside and was running along with some of my friends on the sidewalk when I stumbled and the kid running behind me stepped on my leg. He was a bit over weight and I was skinny and undernourished. When he landed on my leg, he broke it. They sent for my sister, and her boyfriend carried me up to the house. They placed me in bed where I spent the entire night in severe pain.

The next morning our family doctor showed up to prepare me for a trip to the hospital. For some reason I could never understand, he had me stand up while placing a wooden splint on my leg. Why he didn't have me lie on the bed, I could not figure out. This caused me an extreme amount of pain. As young as I was I thought he should have had me lay on the bed as it would have been less painful.

I learned that this doctor's mother and my grandmother came over from Ireland on the same boat, so we always used him for our medical care. He was not the best doctor in the world. I learned later that a young girl who was expecting a baby visited his office. He took out a tape measure and measured her stomach. I believe that was the full extent of his examination. Years later my twin sister visited this doctor concerning a sore throat. She saw him about three times for this same issue and he said you must have your tonsils removed. She asked when he could do this and he said: "I don't remove tonsils from adults, only children". She asked why after three visits he never mentioned this. He was shy and he resembled Stan Laurel of Laurel and Hardy fame which didn't help in developing any confidence. He was assigned to care for my father. He died under his care at the age of 44.

An expression often used by actors is: "Break a leg". Yes, but don't stand up while someone incompetent says he can fix it.

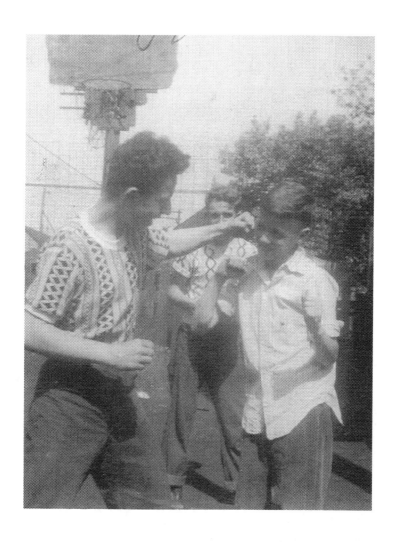

BRUSHES WITH DEATH

When I was growing up in Canaryville, we lived two doors away from a crazy kid. We could always hear his father, who I understood later, was his step-father, was always screaming at him. He was an only child and had plenty of toys on his enclosed back porch and his father would assign what toys were to be played with on certain days.

I have a twin sister and when we were about 4 or 5 years old this kid, Otto, was probably about 10, or 11. He lured us into a shed in his backyard. Fortunately, my mother noticed we were missing and could hear us crying in Otto's shed. I remember my sister crying and pointing at Otto, after we were released, with a terrorized look on her face.

One night my sister and I were sleeping in our bed when the back widow opened and fortunately my sister awoke and ran into my parents' bedroom altering them of the situation. The person opening the window was frightened away and I never woke up. My sister related the story to me the next morning. I have always wondered what would have happened had my sister not awoke.

A few years later when I was about 10, or 11 I walked into Otto's gangway and came upon about three or four dead kittens hanging by their neck off his back porch. This was definitely a person to steer clear of.

Fate intervened in this boy' life, as one night he called a neighbor, Tommy, who lived upstairs of our apartment and asked him if he would like to hitch rides on the street cars travelling on 47th St. Tommy turned him down and the next morning we learned that Otto had been crushed while hanging on the outside of a street car. It was turning a corner and an oncoming streetcar crushed and ripped him accidently off the side of the car.

Otto's wake was not the usual sad affair that most wakes are for young men dying accidently. I think the neighbors, and his family, were relieved with his demise.

I once got hit by a car and thrown onto the asphalt. When my mother showed up at the emergency room the nurse had just emptied a whole bottle of mercurochrome onto my head and it looked like blood from a distance. This was not the best hospital to give any kind of treatment. It had a reputation for big mistakes. It was reported that they amputated a man's leg ----the good one.

I once risked my life swimming in a rapid river that separated Colombia and Ecuador. Another time when we were flying back from Tumaco to Bogota, Colombia we had to change planes in Cali, Colombia and we met some friends at the airport and started drinking and telling jokes. This caused us to miss the connecting flight to Bogota. My friends said not to worry as there would be a flight around midnight. When we boarded the plane the three of us were the only passengers aboard the flight. We had been drinking so much that we all fell fast asleep in our seats. We woke up to hear the stewardesses screaming as the flight had hit a severe storm. We awoke when the plane suddenly lost altitude and causing our legs to rise up, but we soon returned to sleep. The stewardesses were angry with us when we finally made it safely to Bogota. I believed that they felt without the three of us on the flight, it would have been cancelled. Why they didn't just cancel the flight anyway has always been a mystery to me. Another close call came when I was crossing a street in Dublin Ireland. I crossed the street looking the wrong way and about half-way across the street I closely brushed by a truck. It turned out to be a Guinness beer truck. I knew someday the drink would be the cause of my demise, but not this way.

I experienced a near tragedy, but near is not the correct word as I missed this event by 24 hours. I was returning from Greece to Brindisi, Italy with a friend I of mine when we heard that the day before we were leaving the steamship line that we booked our passage had caught fire while out at sea. The next day we boarded our ship and heard all about the fire. These ships hauled automobiles as well and passengers and it one of the cars caught on fire and spread throughout the entire vessel. The captain and the crew deserted the ship leaving all the passengers to see to their own rescue.

Fortunately there was an American Navy vessel operating in the Mediterranean and rescued the people left on board the ship. When we arrived at the Italian port we saw the fire ravaged vessel that had been pulled into the dock and it was scorched. It was severally damaged from the fire. I guess those passengers were every grateful to the U.S. Navy for rescuing them

I guess when we have close calls we learn to appreciate life even more.

JESUS MARY AND JOSEPH

I am a twin, born 11 minutes before my sister Mary. I think I was kicked out early. If you know, or met my sister, you would agree. In the womb Mary got the lion's share of the food she weighed in around 5 or 6 pounds while I weighed less than 4 pounds. I was required to spend a month or more in an incubator prior to coming home.

Catholic hospitals required all girl babies to be baptized Mary and all boy babies baptized Joseph. Thankfully my mother did have me re-baptized and I was named Edward. When my mother finally brought me home, my older brother said Mary looked like a cute baby, while I looked like a chicken. This is something he tells me every year.

Growing up with a sister the same age was difficult. My mother would often restrain me from punching my sister, saying: "Boys cannot hit girls." I was ahead of my time in pushing for equal treatment of women. My sister punched me and I got a black eye. Her fist fit into my eye socket. My mother spoke of this in a proud manner telling people: "Eddie got his first black eye from Mary." She said this as if it were a precious historical moment.

My mother did not cut my hair and I looked more like Mary's twin sister. When we were about five we were invited to a Halloween party at a neighbor's home. My mother got the idea of dressing Mary up as a boy, and putting me in a dress. With my long hair, this was not much of a stretch. I was angry having to dress like a girl and left for the party in a rage. Before I left the house my mother cautioned me not to hit any boys younger than me. I was at the party only a short time when I asked another young boy his age. When he turned out to be the same age as me, I punched him I was dismissed from the party. Later we heard the boy's mother commented how tough that little girl was.

Years later I was reminded of this event when visiting the home of Ernest Hemingway in Oak Park, IL. There was picture of the Hemingway's family in which Ernest had long hair and looked like a little girl. They said his mother wanted twins, so she often dressed him to look like his older sister. Some people thought this accounted for Hemingway's overly aggressive manner.

I had several fights with a young boy in my neighborhood named Jackie. Once when fighting him my mother called me into the house. I was upset with her for doing this, but when I got inside she put a coat on me and sent me back out.

Jackie and I were again fighting when my father came out to watch the fight and started to cheer for Jackie. This upset me so much that I really got aggressive and knocked Jackie to the ground. They carried him into our flat and put him on our couch. He revived when two quarters were placed in his hand. He jumped off the couch and left.

Money was something Jackie always went after. Once we were out trick or treating during Halloween and Jack knocked on doors, received pennies, dimes and nickels. His pockets were full and jingled as he walked. This drew the attention of some older boys who grabbed him and turned him upside down emptying his pockets on to the sidewalk. He was heartbroken.

Years later, a friend told me that Jackie's uncle moved to California and got involved in horse racing. My friend said that Jackie's uncle told him they juiced up a horse and to bet on him. My friend and I went to a local bar and placed a bet on this horse. He lost. A week later my friend got another call and was told the horse was juiced and running again. This time we did not bet. The horse won.

Many years later I heard that Jackie died in prison. I never did get any details, but was not surprised.

DEATH AND BEAUTY

In October 2004 I made a trip with a friend who lives just outside San Francisco. We were planning a trip to Las Vegas for his son's wedding. He wanted to visit Yosemite on our drive to Las Vegas as he said he was beautiful area.

We arrived on a fall day and I indeed was impressed. The weather was warm and we were able to wear short sleeve shirts while walking around the grounds. Yosemite National Park is indeed a beautiful place located in the central eastern portion of the state of California. It covers an area close to 748,000 acres.

I was impressed with the park as I have a hobby of raising Bonsai trees and was really taken by the number of trees that were growing out of boulders. I was surprised how good they appeared as there was not a lot of soil for these trees. I guess all a tree needs is a bit of water and a small amount of soil. That is the basis for Bonsai plants.

As we left Yosemite my friend said that the park could close on short notice. When I asked him for what reason, he said the weather could change and a snow storm could rise up in the park. I was skeptical and asked how in this nice weather a snow storm could possibly develop. But he insisted that it could happen.

I guess growing up in a city like Chicago where the weather is somewhat predictable one can always expect December and January to be cold and July and August to be hot. The weather in Chicago changes, but rarely is the change rapid and extreme.

While driving on the road we heard on the radio that two Japanese people, a man, and a woman died while climbing El Capitan just one day after we left Yosemite. They were near the top of the mountain when the storm rolled into causing their death. It was reported that they were very near the top and close to finishing their climb when the storm hit.

I guess "Mother Nature" can be beautiful and cruel at the same time.

THE BLACKOUT

While performing plays at St. Gabriel's I experienced a strange incident: the director, Lanny Sauris, would direct humorous skits and it was a common practice to end the skits in what's called a "black out". At the end of the skit, (usually right after the punch line) the stage lights would be shut off and the actors would leave the stage until the lights came on again and they started the next skit. This was a common practice that probably went back to vaudeville.

One night there was a young man and woman were on the stage doing a skit and the lights shut down right after at the punch line. Lanny told me later that a local priest rushed up to her quite annoyed and asked: "What is going on? What are you doing."? She was puzzled by his question and asked him to explain himself. He said: "Why are you letting the stage go dark?" She told him that this was a common practice for ending a skit.

He said: "But what do you think people are thinking is going on with that young man and woman when the lights go out?" She said, I don't know Father, what do you think is going on? He was flustered and could not answer and stormed off.

That incident got me thinking about priestly celibacy. I believe the Catholic Church made a big mistake when they decided to introduce celibacy.

In recent decades many priests throughout the United States and Ireland were accused of molesting young boys and girls. The church did nothing to stop it.

When I was growing up in St. Gabriel's there was a young priest in our parish who went on to study Canon Law in Rome. He came back to

America few years later and was put in charge of the priests in the Chicago Archdiocese. Years later, when all these scandals came to light, he was elevated to the rank of Auxiliary Archbishop. At a hearing concerning one of the offending priests, he gave a deposition conducted by a lawyer acting in behalf of some of the victims.

The bishop gave an unreal answer as to why he did not notify the authorities after learning this priest under his command had molested children. He said that he had studied canon law, not criminal law.

I believe the new pope should seriously consider allowing priest to marry discontinuing the celibacy. A result could be that no more priests would wonder what goes with a couple on stages when they are left in the dark. Currently the Catholic Church is in the dark.

HISTORICAL FIGURE

Over the years I have met a few famous authors such as Tom Wolfe, Pete Hamill, Rick Perlstein, James Carroll, a Boston Globe columnist and whose parents once lived in St. Gabriel's parish at the time of World War II. Harold Bloom, Tom Geoghegan who is a Chicago labor lawyer and author. I also met the playwright, Edward Albee. Most of the encounters were brief. Rick Perlstein is the author of several books on politics. He and I worked in the political campaign of Tom Geoghegan who unsuccessfully ran for a seat in congress.

I was most impressed by Pete Hamill as he grew up in a neighborhood and environment similar to mine. It was in Brooklyn and many of the neighbors were people of Irish heritage and there were plenty of taverns. I told him when I met him when he was autographing his autobiography "A Drinking Life" that he was the Studs Lonigan of the East Coast. He liked the comparison.

I once saw the historian William Manchester standing a few feet from me at the Chicago O'Hare airport, but I did not approach him. I saw him the day before on a television show where he sharply rebutted a Japanese man about the war with Japan. In his autobiography "Goodbye, Darkness: A Memoir of the Pacific War." Manchester served in the Pacific and he wrote interesting details of the battles. It was a well written book and I also enjoyed his other books about McArthur and Churchill and later I regretted that I had not approached him and complimented him on his various books.

The most astounding memory I have of seeing someone of significance was just mere chance. I was travelling in Spain and I heard of an incident that took place in Madrid while I was visiting there when an American tourist had recently been caught defacing a poster of General Franco. I was not aware that General Franco was still alive, although he was still respected and protected by the officials of the Spanish government.

My friend and I were leaving Spain and heading back to France and when we were approaching the border we saw a large number of soldiers standing around the hills overlooking the Pyrenees. We learned that General Francisco Franco would soon be disembarking from a ship. We stood on the hillside in the warm summer sun waiting for the General when a small vessel pulled up to the dock and the old man, dressed in a white uniform stepped onto the pier. He was by himself with no escorts and walked to a waiting limousine.

I was surprised to see a character from history that I heard so much about. The Spanish Civil War fought between 1936 and 1939 was always referred to as the "dress rehearsal" for World War II as the opponents were exactly the same governments that were opposing each other in the Spanish Civil War. Close to 3,000 Americans volunteered to fight in this conflict under the name the Abraham Lincoln Brigade. Earnest Hemingway covered the Spanish Civil war as a war correspondent for a North American newspaper.

Whenever I see Picasso's "Guernica" the painting that portrayed the bombing of Spain by the Italian and German air force during the civil war, I cannot help think about seeing General Franco.

The year was 1972 and General Franco was close to eighty and he looked his age shuffling along to his limousine. He died a few years later. This was something I always liked about travelling when I experienced some things unplanned. Seeing the General Franco was one of the unplanned experiences. It was great.

Early in 2015 the Spanish government announced that General Franco was a dictator. Really?

GLACIER NATIONAL PARK

An old neighborhood buddy and I were planning to visit glacier national park in Montana. On the way we stopped in a bar in Naples, Idaho, near the Montana state line for a few drinks, which actually became quite a few. It turned out that the bar was a gathering spot for outdoorsmen and hunters. After a while, the patrons engaged us in conversation asking what we thought of the new law.

We hesitated as we did not know what they were talking about. We soon discovered the new law was the prohibition against killing wolves.

We hesitated to answer, as it was not an issue for me or my friend. He lived in San Francisco and I live in Chicago. This seemed to be a major issue among the patrons of this bar and they were upset. How could the government prohibit them from killing a wolf. There were pictures on the wall of men with wolves and deer had they killed. This was a big topic in that bar. The wolf was not a problem or an issue for us so we left after a while and headed to glacier national park where we did not kill, or even see a single wolf.

ABOUT THE AUTHOR

Ed Flynn grew up in a lower middle class neighborhood on the Southside of Chicago just East of the Chicago Stockyards.

Printed in the United States
By Bookmasters